WHAT IS THE CHURCH?

THE CRUCIAL QUESTIONS SERIES
BY R. C. SPROUL

CRUCIAL
QUESTIONS
No. | 17

WHAT IS
THE CHURCH?

R.C. SPROUL

ℝ *Reformation Trust*   A DIVISION OF LIGONIER MINISTRIES, ORLANDO, FL

What Is the Church?
© 2013 by R. C. Sproul
Published by Reformation Trust Publishing
a division of Ligonier Ministries
421 Ligonier Court, Sanford, FL 32771
Ligonier.org   ReformationTrust.com

Printed in North Mankato, MN
Corporate Graphics
October 2013
First edition

Cover design: Gearbox Studios
Interior design and typeset: Katherine Lloyd, The DESK

All Scripture quotations are from *The Holy Bible, English Standard
Version*®, copyright © 2001 by Crossway Bibles, a publishing ministry of
Good News Publishers. Used by permission. All rights reserved.

Library of Congress Cataloging-in-Publication Data

Sproul, R. C. (Robert Charles), 1939-
  What is the church? / by R. C. Sproul.
     pages cm. -- (The crucial questions series ; No. 17)
  ISBN 978-1-56769-329-4
  1. Church. I. Title.
  BV600.3.S69 2013
  262--dc23

                    2013015788

CONTENTS

Chapter One

THE CHURCH
IS ONE

In the seventeenth chapter of John's gospel, Jesus gives the most extensive prayer that is recorded for us in the New Testament. It is a prayer of intercession in which He prayed for His disciples and for all who would believe through the testimony of the disciples. That prayer is called Jesus' High Priestly Prayer. One of the central themes of that prayer is Christ's request to the Father that His people might be one. It was a prayer for Christian unity. Yet here we are, in the twenty-first century, and the church is probably more fragmented than at any time in church history. We've seen a crisis with the question, "What is the church after all?"

Historically, via the ancient church council of Nicea, the church has been defined by four key words. It is, 1) one, 2) holy, 3) catholic, and 4) apostolic. As we study the nature of the church, I want to look at these four descriptive categories as they define the nature of the church.

First of all, the church is one. Really? If we surveyed the landscape of modern-day Christianity, the last word we might use to describe it would be *one* or *unified*.

How are we to understand and respond to Christ's prayer for the unity of the church and for the ancient church's declaration that the church is one? There have been different approaches to this throughout history. In the twentieth century there was what has been labeled "the ecumenical movement." This was an attempt through the World Council of Churches and other bodies to move in the direction of forming or reforming denominational splinter groups into one centralized, ecclesiastical body. The whole goal of the ecumenical movement was to restore unity to the visible church. One of the things that we saw as a result of this push toward unity was an increasing number of mergers between denominations that formerly were divided. Unfortunately, what often happens when two churches or denominations merge is that certain people don't agree with the merger, and they leave the newly formed organization to create a new organization that aligns with their values. So, in their effort to have fewer churches through unification, these movements simply create more churches.

In addition, another problem has emerged. This is the problem of pluralism. Pluralism is a philosophy that allows for a wide diversity of viewpoints and doctrines to co-exist within a single body. Because so many doctrinal disputes have emerged within some churches, they have tried to keep the peace and unity, and at the same time accommodate differing views within the church. It is an attempt to accommodate conflicting viewpoints.

As the church becomes more pluralistic, the number of contradictory viewpoints that are tolerated increases. In turn, organizational and structural unity become the central concern. People strive to keep the church visibly united at all costs. However, there is always a price tag for that, and historically, the price tag has been the confessional purity of the churches.

When the Protestant movement began in the sixteenth and seventeenth centuries, confessions were created. These were creedal statements that set forth the doctrines that were embraced and confessed by these particular churches. For the most part, these confessional documents summarize the core tenets of what it means to be a Christian—things such as a belief in the Trinity, Christ as one person with two natures, and the bodily resurrection. For centuries, Protestantism was defined by the body of doctrine that was confessed by each organization. But in our day, part of the impact of the ecumenical movement has been the relativizing of these older confessions. In addition, an attempt is made in some churches to broaden the confessional basis along the lines of pluralism in order to achieve the unity of the visible church.

If you are a part of a church, why do you belong there? For quite some time now, I have noticed that people have a tendency to flip between denominations. The tendency is to go where they like the pastor, the preaching, the music, or a particular program. Oftentimes, people feel comfortable moving from denomination to denomination or from church home to church home. Sadly, we rarely find people paying attention to what the church believes. When the church was called to unity in the New Testament, however, we must remember that the Apostle Paul spoke of unity in these terms: one Lord, one faith, and one baptism. This unity is not something that is merely superficial in terms of being a unified organization or a unified methodology, but first and foremost, it is a unified confession of faith in the person and work of Christ. And second, the content of that confession is to be agreed upon. Sadly, the church's unity has been broken precisely where unity is supposed to be found, namely, unity in the Apostolic gospel.

Chapter Two

UNITED
IN THE TRUTH

We have learned so far that there are four main quali-
fications for the church of Christ: it is one, holy,
catholic, and apostolic. We've considered the oneness
or unity of the church, looking at some of the historical
problems that have emerged as a result of the ecumenical
movement. This ecumenism seeks to bring as much visible,
organizational, and institutional unity to the church as it
possibly can. In the wake of that movement, churches have

found it necessary to broaden their theological base and their confessional base in order to accommodate divergent theologies within the institution. This is called pluralism.

There has always been a certain level of pluralism within historic Christianity. I took a course in graduate school called "The History of Heresy." Students had to examine some of the most volatile theological controversies in church history. We looked at the Ebionite heresy, the Docetic heresy, and the Gnostic heresy. We also studied the famous church councils like Nicea and Chalcedon. These councils addressed different varieties of heresy relating to Christology. The church has always had to deal with heresy, and the church has always made a distinction between heresy and error. This is a distinction not of kind but of degree. The church is always plagued with errors or at least some members who are in error in their thinking and in their beliefs. But when an error becomes so serious that it threatens the very life of the church and affects the essentials of the Christian faith, then the church has to stand up and say, "This is not what we believe. This false belief is heresy and cannot be tolerated within the visible church." Historically, that's what has happened with conflicts over theology.

It is important to understand that there are errors that we would call non-essential, that is, errors where salvation is not at stake. For many years Christians have debated the proper mode of baptism. Is it immersion, sprinkling, or pouring? But there are few people in Christian history who would argue that a certain type of baptism is essential to Christianity and to salvation. On the other side of the coin, most Christians will grant that all truth is important and that all obedience in the Christian life is important. Though we differ on certain things, we recognize that we are all trying to be pleasing to God and be obedient to the Scriptures. Even so, sometimes we simply can't agree.

With respect to sin in general, the Bible speaks of a love that covers a multitude of sins. Yet there are also particular sins that are so heinous that they require discipline in the life of the church. In many cases, there are formal trials that can lead to a person's removal from church membership.

In the New Testament, excommunication is not prescribed for every sin that people commit. Instead, love, patience, tolerance, and long-suffering must characterize Christian people. We are to bear with one another's weaknesses in a patient and loving manner. We should not try to make a disciplinary case out of every difference of opinion.

Historically, the church has recognized that there are differences that are not essential to salvation. They don't affect the *esse* (Latin for essence, being, or substance) of the church. There are some issues that affect the very essence of Christianity, and those are the issues that have been debated in the most disturbing controversies of doctrine in the history of the church.

But there's another level. There are those errors that are not necessarily mistakes with respect to the essence of Christianity, but they do reflect what we call the *bene esse*. *Bene* is simply the word for "well" in Latin. So, we're making a distinction between those errors that affect the being of the church (major heresy) and lesser heresies that affect the well-being of the church.

The church has always had a hard time figuring out how to maintain unity and purity. My great fear in this generation is that what we're seeing take place is a kind of ecumenical movement that seeks to neutralize and relativize doctrine. It begins by negotiating a central truth like the deity of Christ or the atonement of Christ—all in the name of visible unity.

The crisis that the church is facing today is largely a result of the impact of the eighteenth-century Enlightenment on the church and the advent of what was called nineteenth-century liberalism. In the past, to be liberal simply meant to be free and open. In and of itself, the term *liberal* describes a virtue. But when you put that suffix *-ism* on the end, it refers to a particular school of theology that has had massive influence on the visible church across denominational lines. It began with German theologians attacking the supernatural dimensions of historic Christianity and denying the validity of biblical miracles. They tried to reduce the Christian faith to a moral code or a system of values. They should have left the orthodox churches and sought to establish a completely new religion because that's what they were actually doing.

But that's not what the vast majority of the liberals did. Instead, they sought to maintain their standing in the visible church by capturing seminaries, colleges, boards, and agencies of the major denominations. By and large they succeeded. So at the beginning of the twentieth century, there was a catastrophic struggle in America that was known as the Fundamentalist-Modernist Controversy.

Churches began to be divided between liberals and conservatives and between evangelicals and modernists. In many cases, liberals and conservatives continued to co-exist within large denominations, but it was anything but a peaceful co-existence. Since then, many of the denominations have split to such a degree that we've seen that mainline churches are not even mainline churches anymore, at least in terms of their size and influence. The growth among evangelical churches has been steadily upward, whereas the mainline churches that were captured by liberalism have been on a downward trend. One denomination has lost more than a million members in just two or three decades.

I'm amazed at how many people seem to have little awareness of the distinctive theology of nineteenth-century liberalism. There still seems to be a public trust of pastors who don't believe in the deity of Christ, the atonement of Christ, or the virgin birth of Christ. Many people, are shocked to learn that in some denominations, almost 80 percent of the pastors deny such things. They ask, "Why would somebody be a minister and not believe in these things?" And I respond that there's nothing new about that. We've had this problem for a long time.

Chapter Three

DOCTRINE
DIVIDES

When I was a young boy, I learned a saying that has served me well. It goes like this: "ornithological specimens of the same or similar plumage tend to habitually congregate in the closest possible proximity." Or being translated, "birds of a feather flock together." We have a tendency to want to congregate with people with whom we hold similar values and viewpoints. In fact, one of the scandals of Protestantism is that many times the church's membership is not defined by a common confession of faith but rather along socioeconomic lines of similarity. One of the things in the past that I respected about the Roman Catholic Church was that the church was established along the parish concept. We don't see a first, second, third, fourth, and fifth Roman Catholic Church on the same block like we might have the First Baptist Church and the Second Baptist Church, or the First Presbyterian Church, the Second Presbyterian Church and the Third Presbyterian Church.

The unity of the New Testament is a unity of faith. The Roman Catholic Church decided to have people from management, from labor, and from various ethnic backgrounds in the same congregation. That's a wonderful practice, because the church isn't to be targeted to some particular demographic group. The whole of society is called to participate in the body of Christ. In the New Testament community, there wasn't a Baptist church in Ephesus and a Presbyterian church in Ephesus and a Lutheran church in Ephesus. It was the church in Ephesus. Of course, very small villages and towns in our day may have only one church, but for the most part, we have a proliferation of churches. But again, the unity of which the New

Testament speaks is a unity of faith, a unity where people come together because of a common commitment to truth and to the gospel. In our day, we have seen attempts to find unity strictly through visible organizational structures. Another way in which we try to define unity is to concentrate our efforts on what may be called spiritual unity.

I remember that in the 1970s, when I was in Pennsylvania at the Ligonier Valley Study Center, we hosted a group of Christians who had come from France to visit us. It was a group of charismatic Christians. They shared their charismatic experience but they were from a wide diversity of ecclesiastical backgrounds. Some were Lutheran and some were Roman Catholic and some were Pentecostal and some were Presbyterian. They talked with great joy and excitement about the unity that they had experienced as being one in the Spirit.

I was amazed at their obvious sense of unity so I said to them, "How have you been able to overcome some of these serious historical differences that you have?" And they said, "Well, like what, for instance?" So I mentioned a couple of them. It was the wrong thing to do, because in five minutes they were at each other's throats over these things. In other words, they were able to have their unity as long as they set aside their doctrinal differences. Can you sense the tension of that? On the one hand, there's something extremely positive about the fellowship and the spiritual unity that was real. But there is serious danger in trying to ignore the doctrinal differences altogether.

That seems to be the drift of our culture today. The axiom for our times is the statement "doctrine divides." It's true historically—doctrine does have a tendency to divide people. Have you ever wondered why it divides? Liberal institutions seem to achieve a high level of toleration for viewpoints other than their own. By contrast, the conservatives seem to fight over many things.

But liberals may not be as tolerant as one might think. They tend to be lax on doctrine until the discussion turns to conservative doctrine. Then they become vociferous against it. Those who pride themselves on being open-minded quickly become close-minded. I believe the basic reason why liberal churches are able to tolerate such a wide variety of doctrines is because doctrine doesn't matter to them much at all. They have no passion about the essential content of the Christian faith, whereas in the conservative milieu people are prepared to give their lives for the truth of the Scriptures because they see these things as having eternal significance.

For those of the liberal persuasion the environment can be very diverse with respect to the tenets of creedal statements of Christianity because it doesn't matter to them. But creeds do matter to believers because believers are concerned about the content of their faith. Believers who are trying to be faithful to the Scriptures know that on virtually every page of the New Testament Epistles there is an exhortation with respect to guarding the truth of the faith once delivered. Paul is very concerned, as he gives advice to Timothy, to Titus, and others, to warn the church about those who would undermine the truth of the Apostolic faith by means of false doctrine.

The strongest indictment against nineteenth-century liberalism was that waged by the Swiss theologian Emil Brunner in his classic work *Das Midler*, or *The Mediator*. In this work, he talked about the Christology developed in nineteenth-century theology that resulted in the denial of the deity of Christ and of His substitutionary atonement. Brunner said that he could define the essence of nineteenth-century liberalism in one word, and the word was *unglaube*, or unbelief. He said that nineteenth-century liberalism was a monument to unbelief.

The most volatile controversy in the history of theology

was the Protestant Reformation of the sixteenth century. This controversy centered around two main questions: what is the gospel? and what must I do to be saved? Martin Luther endured great hardship and the hostility of multitudes of people as the furor of that controversy raged on. Toward the end of his life, Luther observed that the light of the gospel had broken through in his day and lightened the darkness. Remember the motto of the Reformation: *Post tenebras lux,* that is, "After darkness, light." Luther said that it was inevitable that before long, the truth of the gospel would be hidden once more in obscurity. The reason he gave was that where the gospel is preached, it divides and controversy ensues. People don't want ongoing controversy. We want peace.

The message of the false prophets of Israel was one of peace. But their peace was an illusion. They preached peace when there was no peace, or what Luther called a carnal peace. Luther said that when the gospel is preached with passion and with accuracy, it does not bring peace. In fact, our Lord Himself said, "Do not think that I have come to bring peace to the earth. I have not come to bring peace, but a sword" (Matt. 10:34). That does not mean that we are called to use weapons of military combat to further the extension of the kingdom. We are to be peacemakers. We are to be tolerant, kind, and patient people. But if you look at the record of history, the true prophets of Israel contended for the truth, and every time they did, controversy emerged.

Probably no human being has engendered as much controversy as Jesus Christ did. People were galvanized either for Him or against Him. The record of the Apostolic church in the book of Acts is the record of ongoing and unabated controversy. The controversy focused on the preaching of the gospel. So controversial was the preaching of the gospel that the religious establishment of the Jewish community forbade the Apostles from preaching the gospel at all because it was controversial and because it divided people.

In our generation we've been told that the highest virtue is peace. We've lived in the age of the atomic bomb. We've seen widespread warfare. We're tired of disputes, tired of people fighting and killing each other. It is by God's grace that churches aren't burning people at the stake or putting them on torture racks as was done in earlier centuries. We've learned to coexist with people with whom we disagree. We value that peace. But I'm afraid the danger is that we value it so much that we're willing to obscure the gospel itself. We have to be careful of speaking about unity when we really don't have it. At times I think we believe we have more unity than we actually have.

Historically, at the time of the Reformation, the Protestants were not only called Protestants but also "Evangelicals." They were called Evangelicals because they embraced the *evangel*, the gospel. Historically, though the Evangelicals of the sixteenth century started different denominations, there were still foundational principles of unity that bound them all together. The two major points of unity in historic and classical Evangelicalism were two key solas of the Reformation—*sola scriptura* and *sola fide*. *Sola scriptura* reflects the fact that all the different Protestant parties believed that the Bible was the final authority for matters of faith and practice. They all believed in the inspiration and infallibility of the Bible. And second, they agreed on the cardinal issue of the sixteenth century, namely, the doctrine of justification by faith alone, that is, *sola fide*. Wherever else they differed (such as over the sacraments and other doctrines), at least they had the cement of what they did hold in common that bound Protestants together. That unity endured for several centuries.

It's only in our time that we've seen this group of people who call themselves Evangelicals break ranks over these two doctrines. Up until the latter part of the twentieth century, one could almost guarantee that a person who called himself an Evangelical believed that the Bible was the Word of God, that it was infallible, that it was inspired, and that it was inerrant. You can't make that assumption anymore. That unity has been dismantled.

In fact, one historian argues that the term *Evangelical* has been almost entirely emptied of its meaning. Historically, to be an Evangelical meant something doctrinally. That is, it was defined in terms of a particular confession. Now it tends to be defined by a methodology rather than a theology. And there is the same kind of pluralism rampant in so-called Evangelical circles today that we have seen in historic liberalism.

It's a razor's edge to try to live as a Christian, and as much as possible to "live peaceably with all" (Rom. 12:18). We really need to bend over backwards to keep peace. Yet at the same time, we're called to be faithful to the truth of the gospel and the purity of the church.

Chapter Four

VISIBLE AND INVISIBLE

Have you ever heard of term the *invisible church*? The idea of the invisible church was first developed in depth by Saint Augustine. He made a distinction between the invisible church and the visible church. This distinction by Augustine has often been misunderstood. What he meant by the visible church was the church as an institution that we see visibly in the world. It has a list of members on its rolls and we can identify them.

Before we consider the invisible church, let's ask a question: do you have to go to church to be a Christian? Is church attendance, if you're physically able, a requirement to go to heaven? In a very technical sense, the answer is no. However, we need to remember a few things. Christ commands His people not to forsake the assembling together (Heb. 10:25). When God constituted the people of Israel, He organized them into a visible nation and placed upon them a sober and sacred obligation to be in corporate worship before Him. If a person is in Christ, he is called to participate in *koinonia*—the fellowship of other Christians and the worship of God according to the precepts of Christ. If a person knows all these things and persistently and willfully refuses to join in them, would that not raise serious questions about the reality of that person's conversion? Perhaps a person could be a new Christian and take that position, but I would say that's highly unlikely.

Some of us may be deceiving ourselves in terms of our own conversion. We may claim to be Christians, but if we love Christ, how can we despise His bride? How can we consistently and persistently absent ourself from that which He has called us to join—His visible church? I offer a sober warning to those who are doing this. You may, in fact, be deluding yourself about the state of your soul.

The invisible church is sometimes mistakenly thought of as something antithetical to the visible church, something that's outside of, or apart from, the visible church. Augustine didn't think in these categories. Augustine said that the invisible church is found substantially within the visible church. Imagine two circles. The first circle has "the visible church" written on it. That's the outward, humanly perceivable, institutional church as we know it. The invisible church, as another circle, exists substantially within the circle of the visible church. There may be a few people in the invisible church who aren't members of the visible church, but they are few and far between.

Why does Augustine speak of an invisible church? He does this to be faithful to the teaching of Jesus in the New Testament. Augustine taught that the church is a *corpus permixtum*. What does that mean? We know what a corpus is. It's a body. Corpus Christi means what? The body of Christ. Corporation is an organization of people. *Corpus permixtum* means, the church is a mixed body.

Within the physical confines of the institutional church there are people who are true believers, but there are also unbelievers inside the visible, institutional church.

They're in the church, but they're not in Christ because they've made a false profession of faith. Jesus said of some of His contemporaries, "This people honors me with their lips, but their hearts are far from me" (Matt. 15:8). Jesus recognized that there were people within Israel who were not true believers. Paul said something similar: "Not all who are descended from Israel belong to Israel" (Rom. 9:6). These Jews went through the rituals and were part of the visible community. They were participating in all of the activities, but they were still aliens and strangers to the things of God.

In the New Testament, the metaphor that Jesus uses with respect to this is the metaphor of the tares and the wheat. Tares are weeds. The metaphor is a simple one in the agricultural environment. In order to get maximum productivity out of a garden, one has to minimize the tares because they seem to grow more easily than the produce.

Jesus uses this metaphor to give a warning to the church that, on the one hand, the church is to be engaged in discipline so that those weeds that threaten to destroy the purity of the church are removed. He also told us to take great care in exercising church discipline, lest in our zeal to purify the church we rip out the wheat along with the tares.

God looks on the heart and what always remains invisible to me is the soul of another person. I can listen to your confession of faith. I can observe your life. But I don't know what's in the deepest chambers of your heart. I can't see your soul. I can't read your mind. But God can read your mind, and God knows exactly what the state of your soul is at any given moment. What is invisible to me is visible to God. This is a distinction with respect to our limited perception.

Who is in the invisible church? According to Augustine, all those who are true believers. And he referred, of course, to the elect, because all of the elect, according to Augustine, finally come to true faith. And all of those who come to true faith are numbered among the elect. So when he spoke about the invisible church, he was speaking about the elect, those who truly are in Christ and are true children of God.

John Calvin said that we ought not to think of the invisible church as something that is imaginary or lives in a twilight zone. Following Augustine, Calvin insisted that the invisible church exists substantially within the visible church. He said it is the principal task of the invisible church to make the invisible church visible.

What did he mean by that? Calvin was going back to the ascension of Jesus and the last question the disciples asked of Jesus before he departed this world when they asked, "Lord, will you at this time restore the kingdom to Israel?" Jesus said: "It is not for you to know times or seasons that the Father has fixed by his own authority. But you will receive power when the Holy Spirit has come upon you, and you will be my witnesses in Jerusalem and in all Judea and Samaria, and to the end of the earth" (Acts 1:7–8).

This statement made by Jesus is often misunderstood because of our Christian jargon. If a Christian is asked, "What does it mean to witness?" the normal answer given is "to tell somebody about Christ." That's not entirely false. There is a sense in which evangelism is a form of witnessing. But it's not the only form. The purpose of witnessing is to make something manifest that is hidden. Calvin said that it is the task of the church to make the invisible kingdom visible. We do that, first of all, by the proclamation of the gospel—by evangelism. But we also do it by modeling the kingdom of God, by demonstrating justice in the world, by demonstrating mercy in the world, and by showing the world what the kingdom of God is supposed to look like. That means the church is to embody and to incarnate the life of God's Spirit in all that it does so that its good works are not hidden under a bushel, but they are plainly in view. We should bear witness to the presence of Christ and to His kingdom in the world.

There is a danger when we use the terms *visible* and *invisible*. Some people think that if they're in the invisible church it means they can be secret service Christians. But we know that the New Testament mandate is for us to bear witness to Christ, to show forth the light of the gospel, and to make His kingdom visible. And that's what the church is to do.

The church in any environment, in any location, in any generation is always more or less visible and more or less authentic. But even churches can lose their lampstand, and can stop being churches. Churches can become apostate. Denominations can become apostate. Whole communions can depart the invisible church and no longer be true churches.

Are you a member of the invisible church? The invisible church is a church that always enjoys unity because we are truly one with Christ. The point of unification of the invisible church, the thing that unifies and transcends church boundaries and denominational lines, is our being in-grafted into Christ. All who are in Christ and all in whom Christ is, are members of His invisible church. That unity is already there and nothing can destroy it. That doesn't mean that we can rest at that point. It's not that we can simply be satisfied with the unity of the invisible church. We should still be working as much as we possibly can for a genuine unity of the visible church.

Chapter Five

THE CHURCH
IS HOLY

The Nicene Creed states, "I believe in one, holy, catholic, and apostolic church." We turn now to the attribute of holiness as it relates to the church. It's been said in times past that the church is the most corrupt institution in the world. Now that may seem something of an overstatement and an exaggeration, but it can be true depending on how we evaluate corruption. In the first instance, if we simply look at naked evil, then obviously things like organized crime or neo-Nazis may be deemed to be far more corrupt than the church. But if we look at goodness and evil in terms of the sliding scale of moral responsibility, then yes, the church is the most corrupt of institutions. Jesus said, "Everyone to whom much was given, of him much will be required" (Luke 12:48). If we applied that standard to the church, then we would say that the church, of all institutions, is the institution that has received the most benefits from divine grace. In light of the manifold benefits and endowments of grace that we have received as the church and the corresponding high level of responsibility attending that, we could say, relatively speaking, that the church is corrupt insofar as we fail to measure up to the responsibility of our calling.

It seems to some people almost humorous that in the New Testament, Paul frequently addressed believers as "saints." For example, he addressed his epistles to the saints who are in Corinth or the saints who are in Ephesus. The word that is translated saints is the word *hagioi*, which means holy ones. The Holy Spirit is called holy with this same Greek word.

In what sense are members of the body of Christ to be

called saints or holy ones—the *hagioi*? We have to look at the various ways in which people may legitimately be called holy. It begins by understanding the church's vocation. A vocation, of course, is a calling. This word has almost disappeared from our common vocabulary. People today speak of their jobs and of their careers, but it used to be that we all understood that we had a vocation. A vocation meant a call from God to be engaged in a particular enterprise. One would consider their calling to be a surgeon or a farmer or a housewife as a responsibility that has been given to them according to their gifts by God.

The whole idea of vocation is built into the biblical word for church. In the New Testament, the Greek word that is used to translate the word *church* is *ekklesia*. We get the word *ecclesiastical* from that Greek term. If we look at this word and break it down, we see that *ekklesia* contains a prefix and a root. You don't have to be a student of Greek to be able to understand this, because the prefix, *ek,* comes from *ex,* which means "from" or "out of." In addition, the primary root of this word comes from the Greek word *kaleō*, which means "to call." It's very close to our own English word *call*. If we look at the root meaning of the term *ekklesia* in the Scriptures, we see that etymologically, it means something that is called out of something else.

The reason the church is called the *ekklesia* is that the church is the company of people who have been called out of the world by God. After Jesus was born, there was an attempt by Herod to kill the infants and to destroy this newborn king. The angel of the Lord warned Joseph in a dream to flee the land, and they went down to Egypt. After Herod died, it was revealed to Joseph that it was safe to return to Palestine and thus we are told that the Scriptures were fulfilled: "Out of Egypt, have I called my son" (Matt. 2:15), referring to a latter day, ultimate fulfillment of what God did originally with the Exodus. There He called Israel out of bondage in Egypt and adopted the nation of Israel as His son. In a real sense, this vocation of the church begins with this call of God, where He redeemed a nation out of slavery in Egypt. But it goes even deeper than that. The Christian and the church, both Israel in the Old Testament and the church in the New Testament, were not merely called by God out of Egypt but they were called out of the world. Not that they were to leave the planet, but this calling was a calling to holiness. We remember that when God formed Israel, He said

to them: "For I am the LORD your God. Consecrate your-
selves therefore, and be holy, for I am holy" (Lev. 11:44).
Long before Paul wrote epistles to the saints—the holy
ones—at Ephesus, Corinth, or Thessalonica, the idea that
the church was a people that had been called out into holiness by God was already deeply and firmly established in
the Old Testament.

The very word *holy* means to be different or to be set
apart. When one is set apart, the person is set apart from
that which is ordinary or common and directed to something extraordinary, something uncommon. Of course, in
biblical categories, that meant that the people of Israel who
were called to holiness were called to live according to a
different pattern, standard, or manner of living from that
which was commonplace in the world. In other words, this
was a call to godliness, to a different way of living.

The first thing that we have to understand when we look
at the statement *the church is holy* is that the church has a
holy vocation, a holy calling. The church has been set apart
from every other institution and the people of God have
been set apart from the world for a specific mission. They
are to mirror and reflect the character of God. This means
that if we are part of the invisible church, we are called to

be a pilgrim people. That's why the Bible emphasizes that we are sojourners, pilgrims, and aliens in this world.

In addition to this, there's another sense in which the church is called holy. The church is called holy because its members are to be people who have been indwelt by God the Holy Spirit. Everyone who is indwelt by the Holy Spirit is considered holy or set apart in the eyes of God. The church is the institution that God has created visibly wherein He has been pleased to have His Spirit dwell. Keep in mind that the Holy Spirit is not the only spirit that we find in the midst of the visible church. We find evil spirits and we have to test the spirits. But the church is holy insofar as the Holy Spirit is present and functioning in the lives of the people who are there. That's why Paul can look at sinners and address them as saints. In and of themselves they're still sinners but if they have been regenerated by the Holy Spirit, born of the Spirit, and indwelt by the Holy Spirit, they are now the *hagioi*, the "holy ones," those who are in the process of being sanctified.

In response to this, we hear people say that the church is not holy but rather is filled with hypocrites. The reply to that should be, "There's always room for one more." None of us in the church are ever able to live out perfectly the very things that we profess to believe. The believers who are called saints are a fellowship of sinners who are in the process of being sanctified. We are the workmanship of Christ. Christ is molding us and He is molding His church. He is shaping it unto holiness. Just as individuals will not be perfectly sanctified until heaven, so the church will not be perfectly sanctified until the church has been glorified.

We've seen that the Bible refers to the church as "the bride of Christ." One day we will see this bride in her immaculate and breathtaking bridal gown. But right now, the bride's gown is marred. It has blemishes, spots, and wrinkles. But the pledge of Christ to His bride is that He is going to remove every spot, every blemish, and every wrinkle so that in the last day He will present His bride to the Father in the full splendor of perfect holiness.

Right now we are a bride whose dress is wrinkled and spotted. Imagine a bride showing up for a wedding in her wedding gown and you're thinking, "My goodness, she must have had that thing thrown in the corner for the last six months; it's full of wrinkles." No bride would appear like that at her wedding. If we look at the state we're in now, we have nothing of which to boast. Our holiness is in progress, and it is absolutely certain in terms of the destiny of the true church. That doesn't mean that churches as visible institutions won't perish or that churches can't become apostate. They can, but we're talking now about the invisible church. This is the church that is made up of true believers. At some point in history, this church will demonstrate the fullness of her holiness and be faithful to her vocation as she is constantly enabled and purified by the Holy Spirit who indwells her. This is one of the reasons why the church is subjected to great persecutions and to times of great suffering. In that suffering comes the cleansing of the crucible. This is one of the means that God uses to effect sanctification and the purity of the church. From time to time, God is pleased to awaken His people, and we seem always to be in need of awakening to our vocation and calling as the people of God that we might be holy even as He is holy.

Ask yourself the question, "Is my church a holy place?" You may laugh when I ask that because you may be able to point out all the flaws, errors, and sin that invades the church. Remember, the church is still polluted, but it's also the bride of Christ. Holiness is not so much what the church is at any given moment in her history, but what she will be. Our purpose in the present is to be a saint who is being sanctified. In addition, we are to be those who rely upon the gifts and the graces of the Holy Spirit to be faithful to the vocation God has given to the church.

Chapter Six

THE CHURCH
UNIVERSAL

Now that we have considered the unity and holiness of the church, we can move on the the Nicene Creed's third descriptor of the church—the church is *catholic*. It's important to remember that the word *catholic* doesn't refer to the Roman Catholic Church. Rather, the term *catholic* means *universal*, or for all time and in all places. The idea is that the church of Jesus Christ is not a parochial body that is found only in a particular city or only among a unique people that are huddled together in some geographical location. It's not even something that's bound by national borders. Rather, the church of Christ is something that is found all across the world, made up of people from every language, tongue, and nation.

Not too long ago, I spoke at a small church in Florida. There were about a hundred and fifty people in the congregation that morning. I made the comment before I began to preach that I hoped they would excuse me for being nervous about speaking there but that I always got nervous when I preached in front of millions of people. They laughed and looked around to see if there was a radio program being done or a television camera to beam this out beyond the confines of this small church. I assured them that I was serious and turned their attention to a passage from the book of Hebrews. The author writes this:

> "For you have not come to what may be touched, a blazing fire and darkness and gloom and a tempest and the sound of a trumpet and a voice whose words made the hearers beg that no further messages be spoken to them. For they could not

endure the order that was given, 'If even a beast touches the mountain, it shall be stoned.' Indeed, so terrifying was the sight that Moses said, 'I tremble with fear.' But you have come to Mount Zion and to the city of the living God, the heavenly Jerusalem, and to innumerable angels in festal gathering, and to the assembly of the firstborn who are enrolled in heaven, and to God, the judge of all, and to the spirits of the righteous made perfect, and to Jesus, the mediator of a new covenant, and to the sprinkled blood that speaks a better word than the blood of Abel" (Heb. 12:18–24).

The author of Hebrews is speaking here of the church and the experience of the church universal. He reminds us of the new situation that has come to pass with the triumph of Christ and that things have changed since the days of the Old Testament. He says that you don't come to that mountain that was covered with darkness and with thunder and lightning, that was a place of abject terror. (This describes the occasion when God came from heaven to Mount Sinai and gave the tablets of stone, the law, to Moses.) The author says that's not what we're doing when we go to church.

Now when we attend church, we're entering into heaven itself, where Christ has gone in His ascension. As our high priest, He has entered into the heavenly sanctuary once for all and has ripped apart this veil of separation that prohibited access for us into the immediate presence of God. According to this text, we have now been given access to heaven itself.

God is everywhere, He's not just inside a church building. We know we can't restrict His presence, but there is an important symbolic significance at the door of a church. When we walk into that building, spiritually speaking, we are coming to the place where God's people are assembled together to offer worship and the sacrifice of praise to Him. The church is holy ground. It's the sacred place where the people of God are gathered together for the sacred task of worship.

The New Testament says that when we enter into worship together, we're not just worshiping in an assembly of a hundred and fifty people, but our worship is taking place in heaven. Paul warns us of our behavior during the assembly because the angels are watching and participating. Also, the author of Hebrews tells us that we are surrounded by a cloud of witnesses—the saints who have gone before us.

So, who is in our congregation on Sunday morning? Last Sunday I was in church, and guess who was there? Abel, Noah, Abraham, and Isaac showed up, and also David and Deborah and Joshua and Isaiah and Jeremiah and Esther and Amos and Leah and Hosea and Joel and Ezekiel and Hannah and Daniel were there. Paul and Peter were there, as well as Stephen, Mary, Barnabas, and Luke, the great physician. Timothy comes to our church, along with Titus and James. And I looked around, and guess who else was there? I couldn't believe it. Athanasius, Augustine, Martin and Katie Luther, John and Idelette Calvin, Jonathan and Sarah Edwards, and B. B. Warfield. All of the saints who have entered into their rest are part of the heavenly assembly. When the church gathers, no matter how small, no matter how remote the place where it assembles—it is the catholic church.

Not only that, but in our gathering in church we are enjoying what the Apostle's Creed calls the *communio sanctorum*—the communion of the saints. It's not just the saints who have gone before us into heaven—the church triumphant—but the saints who are still here in the church militant: the saints from the Czech Republic, the saints from Hungary, from Romania, from China, from Brazil, from Kenya, from England, and all across the globe. We're joined together in a communion of the church catholic. How can that be? It's very simple. It's the mystical union of Christ and His bride. Everybody who's a part of the bride of Christ is in Christ Jesus. Wherever Christ is, there is His church.

Let's recall the book of Hebrews again:

> "But you have come to Mount Zion and to the city of the living God, the heavenly Jerusalem, and to innumerable angels in festal gathering, and to the assembly of the firstborn who are enrolled in heaven, and to God, the judge of all, and to the spirits of the righteous made perfect, and to Jesus, the mediator of a new covenant, and to the sprinkled blood that speaks a better word than the blood of Abel" (Heb. 12:22–24).

The greatest thing about the church in worship is that the church is in the presence of Christ. Christ comes to his bride, and every time the bride assembles, the bridegroom is there. That's why you don't ever want to miss it. That's why you never want to forsake the assembling together of the saints. If I put out a news bulletin and it said, "Guess who's going to be in church next Sunday? Jesus Himself is coming!" what appointment wouldn't you cancel to be there?

Chapter Seven

FOUNDED ON
THE APOSTLES

What is the foundation of the church? We sing the hymn, "The church's one foundation is Jesus Christ our Lord." Sometimes the words of hymns are conduits for misinformation. Jesus is part of the foundation for sure, but in terms of the building metaphor, we can be more precise. He is not just the foundation but He is called the chief cornerstone of the church. The entire foundation is built in Him as the chief cornerstone.

But what's the foundation? The foundation, according to the New Testament, is the Apostles and the prophets. Remember at Caesarea Philippi when Peter made his great confession after Jesus asked, "But who do you say that I am?" Simon Peter replied, "You are the Christ, the Son of the living God." Jesus answered him, "Blessed are you, Simon Bar-Jonah! For flesh and blood has not revealed this to you, but my Father who is in heaven. And I tell you, you are Peter, and on this rock I will build my church, and the gates of hell shall not prevail against it" (Matt. 16:15–18). The church that Christ established is built not on a foundation of sand, but it's built upon a rock, and the rock upon which it is built, according to the New Testament imagery is the rock of the prophetic and Apostolic Word—the biblical writings.

Consider the book of Revelation. There we read of the vision in chapter 21 of the appearance of the New Jerusalem, the heavenly city that comes down from above. We see that it's described in magnificent terms. In 21:14, we read this, "And the wall of the city had twelve foundations, and on them were the twelve names of the twelve apostles of the Lamb" (Rev. 21:14). Even the New Jerusalem, is based upon the foundation of the Apostles.

What's the significance of this? I think the attribute of the church that is most seriously under attack in our day is its Apostolicity, because there has been a wholesale rejection within the church of the authority of sacred Scripture. This is rebellion against the church's own foundation. You may reject the teaching of Paul, and you may disagree with the teaching of John, and you may not believe in the integrity of sacred Scripture, but I plead with you at this point not to try to steal the church of Christ and build it on some other foundation. Why not have the integrity to say, "I reject Christianity" rather than trying to build a new and improved version on some other foundation?

What does it mean to be Apostolic? To answer that question, we have to go to back to the beginning and ask the question, "What is an Apostle?" The term *Apostle* comes from the Greek word *apostolos,* which means "one who is sent." Apostles are sent from someone to somewhere. In Greek culture, an *apostolos* was somebody who was a messenger, ambassador, or emissary. The *apostolos* was authorized by the king to represent him in his absence.

Since an apostle is one who is sent by somebody and who has delegated authority, the supreme Apostle of the New Testament is Jesus Himself. He was sent by the Father into the world, and He said when He came, "I have not spoken on my own authority, but the Father who sent me has himself given me a commandment—what to say and what to speak" (John 12:49). He also said, "All authority in heaven and on earth has been given to me" (Matt. 28:18).

In this sense, the second Apostle in the New Testament is not one of the disciples (though some of them were Apostles as well) but rather, the Holy Spirit. Jesus said, "And I will ask the Father, and he will give you another Helper, to be with you forever, even the Spirit of truth, whom the world cannot receive, because it neither sees him nor knows him. You know him, for he dwells with you and will be in you" (John 14:16–17).

In the early centuries of the expansion of Christianity, the greatest threat to biblical Christianity came from a heresy called Gnosticism. The Gnostics (from the Greek word *gnōsis*) were those people who claimed to have special knowledge. They claimed to be the *gnōstikoi*, those in the know, and they made a decided effort to supplant the authority of the biblical Apostles. They argued that their knowledge was higher and superior to the knowledge proclaimed by the Apostles of Jesus, and they wrote a massive amount of literature to put forth their claim of superiority.

One of the champions of the Christian faith in that day was a theologian by the name of Irenaeus. Irenaeus was an apologist for Christianity. One of his most important works was titled *Against Heresies*. The chief heresy he addressed was Gnosticism. In his refutation of the Gnostics, Irenaeus used a line of reasoning that's important to us today. That line of reasoning played on the fundamental meaning of the term *apostle*. Again, the word *apostolos* means, literally, "one who is sent or one who is given duly constituted authority to represent the one who sends him." Irenaeus said that the Gnostics not only rejected the authority of the Apostles, but by an irresistible logic, they rejected the authority of Christ and the authority of God.

How did he come to this conclusion? It went like this: by rejecting the Apostles, those who were sent out by Christ and who were commissioned by Christ's authority, they were rejecting the authority of the One who commissioned them. If they were rejecting the authority of the One who sent out the biblical Apostles, namely Christ Himself, then they're also rejecting the authority of the One who commissioned Christ to come into the world, namely, God the Father. In the final analysis, Irenaeus said to the Gnostics that they were godless and their attack on the Apostles reduced to an attack against God Himself because there is a chain of commission going back from the Father to the Son to the Apostles.

The concept of Apostolic tradition is of vital importance to the Bible. This tradition is not some unwritten oral content as is affirmed in non-Protestant Christian traditions, but rather the New Testament itself. It is the Apostolic tradition that the church has not invented, but rather, has received. It received it from the Apostles, who received it from Christ and from His Holy Spirit, who received it from God. That's why a rejection of the teaching of the Apostles is a rejection of the very authority of God.

Chapter Eight

SERVANTS OF THE LORD

The English word *church* comes from the Greek word *kuriakē*, which is a form of the noun *kuriakos* and means, that which is owned or possessed by the *kurios*.

So then, what does *kurios* mean? This is an important word in the New Testament because it is the Greek word for "Lord" and it is the New Testament word that translates the Old Testament covenant name for God—Yahweh—and the Hebrew title *adonai*. When the psalmist says, "O Lᴏʀᴅ, our Lord, how majestic is your name in all the earth!" (Ps. 8:1), he is saying, "Oh *Yahweh,* our *Adonai,* how excellent is thy name in all the earth." When the Greek translation of the Old Testament rendered the term *Adonai,* which means "the sovereign one," it rendered it by the word *kurios.*

Kurios is used in three different ways in the New Testament. In a simple way, the term *kurios* is the polite form of address corresponding somewhat to our word *sir* or *mister.* But the highest and most exalted use of the term kurios is what we call the imperial usage of it, and that is the title that ascribes absolute sovereignty to the one who is *kurios.* Paul used this form of the word in Philippians 2:10–11 when he writes "that every knee will bow and tongue confess that Jesus is *kurios,*" that is, "Lord."

As important as that title is for Christ in the New Testament, I want to look at how it relates to our understanding of the church. Another meaning of the word *kurios* refers to a man in ancient Greek culture who was wealthy enough to own slaves. The slave owner was called a *kurios* and those who were slaves of a *kurios* were purchased by the *kurios.*

I stress that for this reason: *kuriakē* is the etymological foundation of the word *church.* In its original meaning, the church referred to people who were owned by a *kurios*, who were owned and possessed by a lord. In the New Testament, we find this imagery frequently used with respect to the relationship between believers—individually and corporately—and Christ. Paul, for example, calls himself a *doulos,* or *slave*. He uses this metaphor of one who has been purchased. He applies it not only to himself but also to all of the people of God when he says, "You are not your own, for you were bought with a price. So glorify God in your body"(1Cor. 6:19–20). We are God's possession because He has redeemed us.

The New Testament speaks frequently about Christians as being people who are in Christ Jesus. When evangelism takes place, the call to people is not simply to believe *in* Jesus but to believe *into* Him. The Greek word there is *eis*, which means "into." *Eis* and its meaning can be illustrated thus: if I'm outside the city, I have to first move into the city through the city gates before I can be inside the city. That's the idea that we have in the New Testament when we are called to believe into Christ. And when we do have authentic faith, we are in Christ Jesus, and He is in us. This is the mystical union of the believer and Christ.

Now if I have a mystical union with Christ and you

have a mystical union with Christ, that means we have a particular communion, a co-fellowship in Christ. This has all kinds of practical ramifications in the New Testament. For example, Paul tells us that the spirit by which we are to relate to one another in the church is the spirit of charity that covers a multitude of sins. Furthermore, we are called to respect one another's Christian liberty in the Lord. We are to refrain from harsh judgments of each other. We are always to remember that we are relating to people who have been purchased by Christ.

In order to exhibit that kind of attitude toward the people of God and towards the church as an institution, we have to look past the individuals who are plaguing us and who are thorns in our side and look to the One whose church it is. If I am a member of a group of servants and I have conflict with the servants, that conflict must never cause me to speak against the owner of the servants. We are all servants under one Lord.

The hardest and most radical command of Jesus is the command to love our enemies. I can't think of anything more unnatural. If someone is our enemy, the last thing we want to do is promote his welfare and to do good to him. And yet, our Lord said that this is our duty. We must do good to those who spitefully use us and who persecute us. We need to hear this over and over again because to pray for the well-being of those who are at enmity against us is foreign to our basic human nature. And yet, we have the supreme example of Jesus, who laid down His life for the very people who despised Him even unto death. I don't think that we can love our enemies by nature. The only way we can possibly hope to do it is by grace and by looking beyond the enemy to Christ. We are to love our enemies for Christ's sake.

Though fellow Christians cannot ultimately be our enemies, we can still apply Jesus' teaching to church life. If we are to love our enemies, how much more are we to love everyone in the body of Christ?

Chapter Nine

THE MARKS OF
A TRUE CHURCH

When is a church not a church? I frequently get letters from people who pour out their souls and say: "I'm very unhappy in the church I attend. I'm not happy with what's preached or the activities that are going on in the church." This is a very serious question. It was paramount in the sixteenth century at the time of the Reformation, when we saw the greatest fragmentation of the visible church that ever took place. After the Protestant reformers broke with Rome, all kinds of divergent groups arose. They had different creeds, different confessions, different forms of government, and different liturgies. They all claimed to be Christian churches, and many of them claimed to be the only true church. Thus, the people of that day asked: "How can we tell? What are the marks of an authentic church?"

The Reformers wrestled with that question, since Rome did not recognize the Protestant churches as authentic. Rome said in the past that the church can be defined this way: where the bishop is, there is the church, and if there is no authorization by a Roman bishop, then whatever societies spring up are not valid churches. The Protestant Reformers took a different view of the matter. They sought to isolate and delineate the marks of a valid church and they settled on three distinctive characteristics. First, they said a church is a true church when the gospel is preached faithfully. Second, a true church is one where the sacraments are rightly administered. Third, they said a true church practices authentic discipline of its people. A corollary of the third point is ecclesiastical government, which exists for the nurture and the discipline of the people. Of all the different elements that make up a church, these are the three non-negotiables that the Reformers pinpointed as essential marks of a true church. Let's consider these marks in more detail:

1) Where the gospel is proclaimed faithfully. What the Reformers meant by this was not simply the announcement of the good news of Jesus' death and the atonement, but rather the faithful proclamation of the essential truths of Christianity. If a church denied an essential aspect of the Christian faith, that institution would no longer be considered a church. Historic Protestantism would not recognize Mormonism as an authentic Christian church because the Mormon faith has denied the eternal deity of Christ.

2) Where the sacraments are administered. According to the Reformers, if there are no sacraments—the Lord's Supper and baptism—it's not a church. That becomes significant today because we have parachurch groups like Young Life, Campus Crusade, and InterVarsity that are engaged on a daily basis in various elements of Christian outreach and ministry. Their calling is to work alongside the church. Ligonier Ministries may also be called a parachurch ministry. We're an educational institution and we are not a church. Ligonier Ministries doesn't administer the sacraments. We don't have church membership

whereby we impart discipline to people who are part of the constituency of Ligonier. That's not our function. We're called to assist the church educationally, but we have a very narrow focus at that point and don't claim to be a church. Nobody's a member of Ligonier in that sense. We don't baptize people and have them enter the Ligonier church, for there isn't one. The serving of the sacraments is a task for the church.

3) Church discipline. We have seen through church history that church discipline has been somewhat variable. There have been times in the past where church discipline has manifested itself in ways that were harsh. During the sixteenth century, there was fierce persecution not only from the Roman Catholic Church against Protestants, but also Protestants against Catholics. We know that people were subjected to torture and all manner of punishments as a means of church discipline. From our vantage point in the twenty first century, this seems to be cruel, unusual, and barbaric. Perhaps it is, but I want us to understand this: the leaders of the church in the sixteenth century really believed in hell. They believed that there was no worse fate that could befall a human being than to be cast

into hell. The church really believed that it was justifiable to use almost any means necessary to rebuke and discipline its members in order to keep them out of the jaws of hell. If it took a torture chamber, the rack, even the threat of being burned at the stake to rescue a person from the jaws of hell, it was considered legitimate. I'm not defending that, but I am trying to help us understand the mindset of people in the sixteenth century who took hell seriously. Today, we seem to have an attitude that we don't need to discipline people at all because it doesn't matter. That may be because many people don't believe in the threat of divine judgment.

The pendulum tends to swing to extremes in church history when it comes to discipline. Sometimes the church gets involved in harsh and severe forms of discipline. At other times, the church is marked by an extraordinary form of latitudinarianism. This is where no discipline is imposed upon the people. A few years ago, one of the mainline denominations in America had a controversy in the church when a group of pastors and scholars put together a paper in which they completely redefined the Christian sexual ethic of one man and one woman for life in marriage. This report was introduced as legislation for the church amidst much opposition from those who were more orthodox. A showdown came at the annual meeting of this denomination and when the vote was taken, the proposal was defeated.

But what took place after was perhaps more strange. Though the church did not adopt this particular position on sexual behavior, it also did not censure or discipline those who advocated the position. The church was in effect saying, "This is not our official position, but if you want to be a minister in our denomination and hold and teach these things, we're not going to do anything about it." There was a failure of discipline at that point. This happens all the time in the modern-day church.

This also raises a question. If a church fails in a significant way to discipline its members with respect to gross, heinous, and egregious sins, is that institution still a church? When does the church become apostate? That is not an easy question to answer because it's very rare in church history that an institution will admit it doesn't believe in the atonement of Christ or the deity of Christ or other essential truths. It's not always very clear cut. Often, the church plays loosely with essential truths of the Christian faith.

We make a distinction between *de facto* apostasy and *de jure* apostasy, between *formal* and *material* apostasy. Formal apostasy is when the church clearly and unequivocally denies an essential truth of the Christian faith. *De facto* apostasy is apostasy at a material or practical level, where the creeds are still intact but the church doesn't believe the creeds anymore. The church undermines the very creeds that they say that they believe.

That brings us to a practical application. When should one leave a church and go to another? First, I would say that this is not a decision anyone should make lightly. It's a serious matter. Almost always, when we join a church, we do it with a solemn vow before God. To remove oneself from a group before whom one has made a sacred vow requires serious reasons. This must be justified on solid grounds.

Today, people move from one church to another without a second thought. When we leave a church over silly reasons like paint colors or an offending remark, we fail to see the sacred nature of the church itself.

We should not leave when there's no just reason. We ought to honor our commitment to a church to the best of our ability as long as we possibly can unless we are not able to be nurtured and nourished as a Christian there. When the church is apostate, a Christian must leave. You may think you should stay within the church and try to work for its change and recovery, but if the church is in fact apostate, you're not allowed to be there. Consider the showdown between the prophets of Baal and Elijah at Mount Carmel. After God displayed his power over Baal can you imagine somebody saying, "Well, I see now that Yahweh is God, but I'm going to stay here in the house of Baal as salt and light and try to work for its reform"? We're not allowed to do that. If the institution we are in commits apostasy, it is our duty to leave it.

No matter what, we should always look carefully at the marks of the church. Is the gospel preached? Are the sacraments duly administered? Is there a biblical form of church government and discipline? If those three things are present, you ought not to leave. You ought to work to be an edifying part of that section of the body of Christ.

In these few chapters we have glimpsed the nature and scope of God's bride, the church of Jesus Christ. It is only when we understand our true purpose that the church will shine in all of her beauty. United in truth as we hold to the Apostolic faith, we will declare and demonstrate to an onlooking world that our triune God is worthy to be worshiped and served. As the called-out ones of the Father, this is our greatest joy. This is the church: a people for His own possession who live together to glorify Him.

About the Author

Dr. R. C. Sproul is the founder and chairman of Ligonier Ministries, an international Christian education ministry based in Sanford, Florida. He also serves as co-pastor of Saint Andrew's Chapel, a Reformed congregation in Sanford, and as president of Reformation Bible College. His teaching can be heard around the world on the daily radio program *Renewing Your Mind.*

During his distinguished academic career, Dr. Sproul helped train men for the ministry as a professor at several theological seminaries.

He is the author of more than eighty books, including *The Holiness of God, Chosen by God, The Invisible Hand, Faith Alone, A Taste of Heaven, Truths We Confess, The Truth of the Cross,* and *The Prayer of the Lord.* He also served as general editor of *The Reformation Study Bible* and has written several children's books, including *The Prince's Poison Cup.*

Dr. Sproul and his wife, Vesta, make their home in Longwood, Florida.

Further your Bible study with *Tabletalk* magazine, another learning tool from R.C. Sproul.

....

TABLETALK MAGAZINE FEATURES:

A Bible study for each day—Bringing the best in biblical scholarship together with down-to-earth writing, *Tabletalk* helps you understand the Bible and apply it to daily living.

Trusted theological resource—*Tabletalk* avoids trends, shallow doctrine and popular movements to present biblical truth simply and clearly.

Corresponding digital edition—Print subscribers have access to the digital edition for iPad, Kindle Fire, and Android tablet devices.

Sign-up for a free, 3-month trial
of *Tabletalk* magazine
and get *The Holiness of God*
by R.C. Sproul for free.

Go online at TryTabletalk.com/CQ